North Of Your Expectations

Poems Inspired by the Sun

Kenya Wheatley

/ BookLeaf
Publishing
India | USA | UK

Made with ❤ on the BookLeaf Publishing Platform
www.bookleafpub.in
www.bookleafpub.com

Dedication

for lilith,

my reason for everything

Preface

This book is a collection of moments that have been
waiting to speak in other places.

Over the last decade, I've created and carried these
poems with me. Through open mics and late-night
writing sessions, through classrooms and coffee shops,
through love found, love lost, and love remembered.
Most of them were first spoken into rooms full of
strangers or coffee shop regulars who became reflections
of myself, where poetry and art wasn't just written; it
was lived.

Each poem was written to be felt out loud. To move air.
To move energy.

They're stories of love and alignment, of falling into the
self and into others. Of divine timing—that mysterious
rhythm that keeps showing up, reminding me that
everything—every detour, every heartbreak, every spark,
is all part of the plan.

The sun has always been my compass. Its rise and fall, its
warmth and radiance, its distance and consistency; all of
it reminds me of rebirth & reflection. These poems orbit

that light. They were written in reverence to the beauty of what is meant, what is missed, and what still finds its way back to us. All strung together by Love.

This collection is dedicated to my daughter, **Lilith.** My eternal reminder of light and legacy. May she always know that everything that happens is divine and on time, meant to lead her toward her highest aligned truth.

I hope as you read, you feel something familiar. Like sunlight touching your skin.
Something that reminds you that you, too, are part of this great unfolding.
That you are always north of your own expectations.

Acknowledgements

First and foremost, to my daughter **Lilith.** Thank you for giving me a reason to root myself in purpose, to create something that outlives fleeting moments. You are my reflection of love in its purest form, my reminder that light continues through legacy.

To my **family and best friends,** thank you for embracing every layer of me. My curiosity, my eccentricities, my late-night tangents about energy, love, and the universe. Thank you for holding space for me when I needed to rediscover who I was becoming.

To every **lover** who crossed my path: the exes, the almosts, the fwb's, the karmics, the soulmates, and the twin flames. Thank you for showing me the many faces of love and reflection. Each of you taught me something about surrender, divine timing, and the art of transmutation. You were my mirrors and my muses, and your energy helped shape these pages.

To my **future, timeless love,** the one currently on their way. I already thank you before knowing you. Somewhere in these poems, your name hums quietly between the pages with the utmost care and understanding. I've finally learned to say goodbye, in order to say hello to *you*.

To the **coffee shops and sacred spaces** that gave me stages to grow— places like **Klatch Coffee** and others that offered their warmth and walls to the sound of my voice, thank you. And to **The Reverse Orangutan**, for letting me turn your space into a sanctuary of sound, community, and connection. I am forever grateful.

To **A Verbal Coliseum**, the student organization I helped create at UC Riverside with beloved comrades. And to all the **poets** who've ever stood beside me, mic in hand, heart on sleeve. Thank you for reminding me that words build worlds, and that vulnerability shared is power multiplied.

To everyone who's ever listened, complimented, snapped, nodded, or simply felt something while I spoke. You are part of this story too.

Every person, every moment, every heartbreak, every sunrise & sunset has led me here.

All in divine timing.

This World is Better With You

Yes, you
You're already here
So what else can you do
Besides what you've already done
Move me to tears?
Remove my fears?
Give me a reason to peer
Into a life that didn't ever have you?
It's impossible
You're improbable
Yet, you're already here...
Yes, you
This world is better with you

So many aspects
Are nonexistent
Without you in it

Grateful for the lessons already
Show me how to choose me daily
You are your own
Could never be mine
And I like it

No I love it
Exactly like that

Doing That Thing Again

I'm doing that thing again
The thing that tells me
that this is what's right
The thing that tells me
at least you ain't gotta fight..
Yet I feel like I'm fighting for my fucking life

This thing..
is king —
at telling me "you're fine"
But when I step on the floor
I'm walkin this *very* thin line
So fine
it almost doesn't exist.
A line that separates:
Being from doing

Doing is RULED by that thing..
Doing is doing everything it can
To be the man successfully running the show
Yet stressfully taking on other peoples loads
Doing is doing everything it can
To be the woman of his life
Yet causing the misconstruction

Of both new and similar strifes

Doing is perpetually running systems in its head
With its
Infinite illusions of capability—
Yet, abusively abysmal of its potential.
Charmingly chipper just to chug through another day—
yet invincibly ignorant, indecisive, and internally pained.

While
Being lies beneath the surface instead
Being is too busy being the formed foundation of this
shaky shed
Its not attending to the thorny rose garden, or making its
bed
Being ain't got time for Doings insecurities it said
Being only has time for inspiring selfish self care
and selflessly loving on duality
The dualities of life
Because what else is Being if it's not we
What else is Being if it doesn't sing
You
and me.
Because really, we,
Are both one in the same.
I mean that with all the levity
of light-hearted truth

I mean that with all the breadth and brevity
of your one breath and tune
I mean that with all the certain sincerity
That ALL of time just-so-happened to collapse into a
single YOU

So why am I doing that thing again?
Where I anxiously avoid my Self like the plague
Where I literally lose my mind and can't seem to
properly gauge...
What would Being do?

I guess I'm out of practice of attending to my
foundations
I guess I'd rather let the weather rain over me
Then let Love reign instead
Honestly—
I act like I dread the possibility of my Truth
I feel like I'd rather see you recognize the promise of You
I know I should actualize myself more before I start to
impart wisdom out the blue
Or at least I *think* that's how it should go
But there's no telling if I do..
Only one telling is the God in you

So why am I doing that thing again?
Hm..

If I know that life has its basis in Being
Knowing that its energy gives rise
To all that we're seeing...

So why am I doing that thing again?
The thing that evades living a more aligned life
Yeah, that thing..
I guess I'm trying
I guess I'm writing
I guess I'm not totally defeated
sigh
I guess I'm here..
I guess I'm sighing
And hopefully coinciding
With the concept that I am Doing *and* Being
All at the same time

Maybe dharma
lives within these words
Maybe believing in divinity
Lies in the gap of each
and
every
Sound
I make..
Maybe there's more activity.. more energy..
That lies between the space

of each of these words —
Maybe there's more rest.. more life..
That lies outside of this verse

Maybe Love lies at the end of this piece
Maybe Hate hides in the unhealed confines of my mind
Maybe order can only exist while holding hands with
chaos
Maybe I can only live if I continue to die
Maybe blissful states
take refuge
somewhere in the battleground
that is my day to day

And maybe that's all the Peace that I need for now..

Little blips and microchips
of knowing,
and Being known.

& Maybe that's more than enough—
Enough to be seen,
and be shown.

"How are you?"

There goes that question again..
"How are you?"
She's been asked an infinite number of times
How you been? How you doin? How's school? You
havin' fun?
But she ain't ever been asked like this before..
He asked her, How's the sun?

You see, she's been called sunshine one two many times
in her life.
She was beginning to believe that that's all she was.
What a sweet lie, covered in sin,
Light rays infused in her sun-kissed skin.
But just below the surface, graced her darkness within
Yet to everyone else, she could *def* be a sun...
So she turned into a sunrise & sunset all mixed into one.
Full of beginnings and endings
But sun nonetheless.
So when he asked her how the sun was?
She replied..
due to recent rainfall,
Gloomy,
overcast at best

But now
The day is much too blinding for her.
She's been glowin in the luminosity of the moon, for all
to see.

Her moon is private, puzzling, and pieces you back
together.
If she was sun all the time, you couldn't stand sleepin in
her shelter

So she's been submerged in the blues
Of a dark blue hue painted amongst the black skies.
Dancing in the moonlight, unfazed by sunlight
It's the only way she could see his private, puzzling, &
piercing eyes

& Behind her smile, he felt her moon glowing within.

And there goes that question again..
"How are you?"
He's been asked it an infinite number of times
How you been? How you doin? How's work? Any new
tunes?
But he ain't ever been asked like this before..
She asked him, how's the moon?

You see, he's been walking around like moonlight minus

the moonshine
Not fumbling around while dreaming of revelry
He cares enough to maintain his crown,
while progressing toward his personal melody
A quiet as night compression of all his mistakes past
Who knew that blackness was always born to last
Cause just below the surface was born a tireless heart
built to surpass
All the lumps of lovers,
the marks of mothers,
and the scars self inflicted

She wanted to show him the sun she sees shining within

So when she asks him, how the moon is?
He'll reply...
"It's a clear calm night, full of shooting stars,
So serendipitous I made a wish..
That I could meld with the sun forever.
and one day we'll reminisce,
About the time we shared our eternal kiss..
Ive been the moon for so long,
That I made the sun a song,
So she'll never forget
That we were partners all along."

And now,

The night is much too dark for him
He's tryna flicker in the shimmer of her fluorescent skin

His sun is bursting, blazing, & burns a path lighting our
futures
If he was the moon all the time, she couldn't heal his
scars and sutures

So there they were...
Standing there, like the sun and the moon.
He's soaking in some hope
And she's hoping for some faith
Yet every time they're together
The day and night never break

Because the sun is endlessly enamored by the moon
and the moon is forever enraptured by the sun

All my life I've been waiting for you,
A you that's devoted to setting and rising—
Just like I do,
cause yeah,
me too

Wreck Me

How could I admire someone more when the sun comes
up
Exposing them for all that they are,
all that they were through the night,
all the things I couldn't see.
Don't you see?,
even those self inflicted shortcomings,
they're non-existent to me

Your hand, when it brushed across my face
My eyes batted so boldly and so intimately, as if made
from lace
I swear, you wanted that effect to be a replaying cameo
in my mind,
titled "my life meeting yours"
Your touch, whispered appreciation into my skin and
adoration into my hair
As if reaching for my mind, your touch was unfair
But I'm sure, that for the first time in my life,
my eyes sighed the sweetest smile.
And only closed with a longing to open again,
and catch those gracious eyes upon my grin
My grin, softly pursed into a relaxed position
Peaked up, at a single corner, to match yours in

repetition..
I think we smiled at each other the same,
I think we smiled at each other enough to go insane,
I think I want to smile upon that face again

With an aptitude of mutual affection
And an attitude of utmost satisfaction
How dare you place those lips upon mine.
I told myself that we were one in the same,
lip to lip would be the equivalent of not one, but two
lames
But boy, you've got a reckoning with me
& Those all too kind lips are gonna be the wrecking of
me
Destroy my past, but please, help me build my future
I don't need your help, but damn, you *might* make it
better

You see yourself the way that I see me
But believe me when I say, be careful with my seams
They seem to bust at the touch of your fingers treading
through my hair
If you could see the campfire in my heart, I think you'd
love to sit and stare
So believe me when I say, be careful with my seams,
They seem to bust at the thought of you pursuing your
dreams

There is nothing more I want to see then you succeed
I love who you are now, and who you ought to be.
But please, remind me, if and when I focus on you more than me.
Because sometimes I care too much about others before myself.
While I am a natural born queen, the throne I sit upon is of wealth.
Everything I touch does indeed turn to gold..
Mirror to mirror, a reflection of me untold
Millions and millions of words left unsaid,
Yet billions and billions of good feelings left on read

So if I could tell you one thing right now in this very season,
It's that I think you happened for a very good reason.

Reinvent

How could I admire someone more when the sun comes
up
Exposing them for all that they are,
all that they were through the night,
all the things I couldn't see.
Don't you see?,
even those self inflicted shortcomings,
they're non-existent to me

Your hand, when it brushed across my face
My eyes batted so boldly and so intimately, as if made
from lace
I swear, you wanted that effect to be a replaying cameo
in my mind,
titled "my life meeting yours"
Your touch, whispered appreciation into my skin and
adoration into my hair
As if reaching for my mind, your touch was unfair
But I'm sure, that for the first time in my life,
my eyes sighed the sweetest smile.
And only closed with a longing to open again,
and catch those gracious eyes upon my grin
My grin, softly pursed into a relaxed position
Peaked up, at a single corner, to match yours in

repetition..
I think we smiled at each other the same,
I think we smiled at each other enough to go insane,
I think I want to smile upon that face again

With an aptitude of mutual affection
And an attitude of utmost satisfaction
How dare you place those lips upon mine.
I told myself that we were one in the same,
lip to lip would be the equivalent of not one, but two
lames
But boy, you've got a reckoning with me
& those all too kind lips are gonna be the wrecking of me
Destroy my past, but please, help me build my future
I don't need your help, but damn, you *might* make it
better

You see yourself the way that I see me
But believe me when I say, be careful with my seams
They seem to bust at the touch of your fingers treading
through my hair
If you could see the campfire in my heart, I think you'd
love to sit and stare
So believe me when I say, be careful with my seams,
They seem to bust at the thought of you pursuing your
dreams
There is nothing more I want to see then you succeed

I love who you are now, and who you ought to be.
But please, remind me, if and when I focus on you more than me.
Because sometimes I care too much about others before myself.
While I am a natural born queen, the throne I sit upon is of wealth.
Everything I touch does indeed turn to gold..
Mirror to mirror, a reflection of me untold
Millions and millions of words left unsaid,
Yet billions and billions of good feelings left on read

So if I could tell you one thing right now in this very season,
It's that I think you happened for a very good reason.

Peace is Still

It's awful windy out today
But Peace,
You are still
And although things around me
Are turbulent
And windy
Peace is still
And although I may be like the wind
Also turbulent
Also windy
Peace is still still
So I shall learn to be
As well and at will

Be still and know that I am Peace
Be still and know that I am
Be still and know
Be still
&
Be

Fancy

Tell me what it is you want to tell me
But instead of it being in that one line
Make it two
Split up your spitting game
And make it move
I want to dance to what you have to say
Make it a couplet
Make it a haiku
Make yourself a sonnet
And bring me something new
Say it three times so you feel it
And I can feel it too
Don't you see that I won't hurt you?..

I just wanna keep hearing what you have to say
If you didn't limit what you may
I want you to use words you've never used before
I want to be able to discern the dissonance from the
harmony you roar
Explain your truth like you've never known a lie before
Walk in your purpose like how you know that your
worth more
I want you to pretend that no ones ever hurt or blocked
you before

I want you to use words that make your feelings soar
And not sore like you have an injury
Because to take that pain away
I swear I'll make it the death of me

I just want you to...
Tell me everything you want to tell me!
But instead of saying it plainly
I want you to make it fancy
I want to hear words of the rich fall across your lips
So much so that your breath drips in gold
So even when you're sleeping passive
Your waking world leaves gems that are massive
Because we have no time for static
And in any way we grow, we make it expansive
Don't you know that you're attractive?
Yes, attractive. But you also attract what you need and
what you want
I wouldn't write these words and talk this way to a soul
that would front

But to be honest,
I really just want to hear what you have to say
No matter what direction you may sway
Or how your mood has changed your way
To hear you speak is the most simplest of my joys these
days

But I haven't had the pleasure to hear that sweet noise in phase
And to know how you feel, my thoughts are no longer dismayed
I won't have to stumble over the bonds I have created
I'll hold on to the thought of your love like I knew it was fated
And even though many of my nights include getting faded
I hope you trust and believe that my reality isn't jaded
Because in my book, you've never been overrated
And if you're rocking with me
I know your consummated
And persuaded
To be your own personal greatest
And at the end of the day
It's never goodbye,
It's see you later
We'll cater
To each other
Be there
For one another
In the future
Together

Just tell me what you want to say
We can let go of the past

And heal
today

Untitled

I want a love so serious
that I'm not taken seriously at all.
Because I tend to stumble over my words
as if your lovely voice just tied together my shoes.
So every time you speak I trip and fall for you.

I want a love so real
that everything fake in this world bows before it.
A testament to our reality
and how we adore it

I want a love so formed and developed that I become
formless in its hands,
A love where I shape shift into play dough,
mold into desire,
transform into liquid,
and sublimate into air
that weaves in and out of times cloth.

I want a love that inspires perspiration through hard
work.
Because yes,
this is work, and you and I are scheduled to be here.
With each other.

In this place.
For hours at a time.
And the only moment we must part is when our other
responsibilities call.
And when we answer the call,
they swear to let us to return to each other;
having gained a story to share, fruit to bare,
and love that's more deep and rare.

I want a love so free
that we hold no expectations for one another
Because love never limits
what are souls have discovered

I want a love so true,
that if you were to hook me up to a lie detector test
You could see my transparency
and how I could never lie to you like the rest

I want a love so natural
that when you go to the grocery store
you'll see us sitting on a shelf in the organic aisle
And I don't care if we rot—
because what won't expire was the love that made us.
We won't need preservatives to maintain something
ordained in us.

I want a love so right that when youre wrong, I still
chalk it up as a W
Because there's nothing wrong with learning a new way
to love you.

I want a love so pure
that the polluted smog above our heads
cowers to the ends of the earth at first sight
Yes. Our love is going to heal.
Not just each other,
but the world that surrounds it.

I want a love where we never celebrate holidays,
because being loved by you is the real gift that keeps on
giving

I want a love so playful
that when we see eachother,
our spirits collide,
run down the street,
trip over untied shoes,
and scream over soccer and ice cream

I want a love like Hip Hop and R&B
Tunes Like Ja Rule and Ashanti
I want a lo lo lo love like this
Gotta be something for me to write this

Type of love
But I don't mean that Common type of love
I mean that Bobby Caldwell type of love
Because there is a light that shines
Special to You
And Me.

Colors

I appreciate you for showing me your true colors.
But I asked you for something far less complex.
Captivating with clarity,
Soaking in sincerity,
Initiated with integrity.
'Cause it's easy to be a color;
it's a side effect to observing opaquely.
But to be clear and concise with your intent,
you transcend to
Transparency.

Loving Eye

Re-see the environment with a loving eye
You are neither low nor high
You are mere poetry in motion
You are sand on beach, wave in ocean
Like air, you are everything and everywhere,
And all with no compare

Summer Love

I can call it love
If only it begins with summer
Summer love—
Give me that good summer lovin'
Hot and heavy
Lovin' is rainin over me
Keeping me hip and hydrated
Lovin' is rainin over you
Scent of rose hips never outdated
Lovin' is rainin over us
Hip to hip like flower and tree,
stay faded
We're never *too* jaded
Just two honey dips
Looking for tastes that lingers,
Dipping dripping fingers into
Fields of sunflowers
Plant my seed in the pot of your potential
Promise, you will never be sad again

Throw myself through a ringer
To readjust my mind
Cause honey I can't give you all my time
We can't be blind!

Unless we're blinded by the sun
Because summer is upon us
And it's asking this heat to be subjective with me
Theres no good rhymes for objectivity
Bodies speak in vibes,
but the tongue can speak in ties
Come on now sunny,
You know you feel me
Get to know the real me
May not know how to deal with me
But at least we don't tell no lies,
So we tellin' enough just to get by..
Enough to make me ease my mind
Sear my skin like you're brandin' thighs
'Cause I can be this seasons Ruth
The light is my companion
and it always sheds the truth
That two don't *have* to grow to be one
Summer is here and my heart is undone
So, when the cycle turns once more
And sun breaks dawn to hit the shores
Seasons change and leaves will fade
Be sure to come back and walk my way,
Ill be your Summer in November babe

Glass Heart

Over-filling cups
A testament of my love

Rough day?
My elixir's called Pain Away

Dead nights
Who am I?

Ugly Existential
Beautifully Quiet
Charmed smiles
break the silence

Dare you to hold me to the light
Water spots and lipstick marks
Embellish my glass heart

Stains of past sippers
I haven't buffed out

For I have no hands
But I have your lips pressed upon my glass

Sip me empty,
lick me dry,
patiently waiting
for the right amount of care
to clean this glass pristine & fair.

Transmute

I'm so inspired. I'm so grateful. I'm so appreciative. I'm
so in love.

Of the makings of
my mind,
heart, &
soul.

I'm glad I know what it feels like to be so separated from
self
that my homecoming was celebrated.

I'm glad that I experienced the festering of lies,
so that I may indulge in the rejoicing of truth.

I'm glad I've succumbed to the shame of being a horrible
person,
so that I could know & understand what it is to be a
genuinely good one.

I'm glad I fell in love with someone who couldn't love
me in return of equal magnitude,
so that I could learn what it means to love
unconditionally.

I'm glad that I chose to love someone who loved me
more than I loved myself,
so that I may see more clearly my own worth.

I'm glad that I fell for creative, poetic, and musical souls,
so that I could stand up for my own.

I'm glad that I know what it feels like to be used for
superficial desires,
so that I could learn about the bare minimum and look
beyond it.

I'm glad that I've felt the grief of abandonment,
so that I could discover that I'm never truly alone.

I'm glad that I've felt bottomless pits of betrayal,
so that I may see all the ways that I first betrayed myself.

I'm glad that I took the time to grieve what could've
been,
so that I could reconvene and take salvage in what
should be.

I'm glad that I know what it is like to carry a life and not
be able to meet it,
so that the day that I am blessed to do so, I can look life

in the eye...

And guide it by everything I know.

Inspired by the creatives.
Grateful in the face of grace.
Appreciative of the unappreciated.
Loving the unloved.

—

My story is my story. It may not be like yours. But I'm sure that if you read it, and truly read it, from beginning to this current chapter, there is nothing in it that wouldn't make sense. And the same if I read yours. No matter the seemingly mindless behavior I acted upon, no matter the outwardly irrational engagements, no matter the severity of the helpless and hopeless moments. It will make sense. And even after it all, there is no page that I wouldn't have wrote to get to where I am at now. And I won't change that perception for the rest of my book. I choose to read every word and grow in the depth of each single choice of diction that my life has to offer me. I am grateful. I am prepared.

F
  a
      l l
 i
    n
      g

Now is this what falling feels like?
Like you're absolutely scared for your life?

Seems we can predict the future
Sew us up with love sutures

I want to love you recklessly
Without it being the death of me

So I'm ripping and running and falling to pieces.
Fumbling into my fate
because a falling love has no leashes

I could only continue to fall for you for so long
Before I realized, the only thing I fell for was life's

intoxicating song

I fell for you for so long
So now, "so long"

Hello

You can see it in her eyes
She don't got time for goodbyes
Only ever say Hello
Even when her paths aglow
To step foot,
in a new direction

Evolution in the Flesh

I am evolution in the flesh
It only takes a day of my igneous rock
to cool to perfection of ingenious writer's block
It only takes a second of my sedentary moves
To crumble beneath the fist of sedimentary grooves
I am no cool calm collected pile of rocks to sit on your
shelf
I am a gem, a jewel, a crystal. Something of substance,
something of wealth
A woman once told me that crystals are not a solid, nor a
liquid or gas
But merely a billion buzzing particles travelling the
speed of light in pass
Becoming the enchanted,
enhancing the didactic.
Travel your path to become all that you can be
Amplifying the light to augment all you can see

Smitten

You want to love me boldly
I can tell
By the way you look in my eyes
Unthreatened

Many others have tried
And failed
Leaving me to look at their profile
Forgotten

Now I'm the one who shy's
Not strayed
Because I'd like to believe I'm bold
Smitten

Can I love how you deserve?
Thoughts dismayed
To love me is to bear armor
A Battalion

Come for my love, With fists swinging
These walls are much too high to sit upon
But brick by brick, it'll come down singing,
"Is it okay to love again?"

I am pain in the flesh
Beaten bones, no mesh
Break me down with honesty
Hope you visualize the God in me

I Shouldn't Have Left You

Who is the One
that writes these words?
With confusion brewing
through eternal longing

The one who walks in speed
in search of tool to scratch
Who connects the pieces of this poem?
in hopes to connect a piece of the totem

Like a babe released
from maternal womb,
Like a hermit who's forced
to leave his room

Where does the air go
when it leaves the lung?
Craving to find unity
with a song to be sung

The ripped off piece of the
whole desires its true source
The maple bark of a tree
must run its full course

Excavated of its past
and bound to guitar
The wood can't recall even
its maple leaf from afar

Through the strumming of a perspective
the wood tells its journey through a tune
Its life, its past, its want for its roots;
it's like sky that calls for floating balloon

Pity the one who pretends
to not hear its sad song
Because the hollow notes that play
speaks of bliss that comes far along

It's the mere duality of life,
that laughs at the mundane of its strife,
and for all that it cries,
it sings its final goodbye's,

"I shouldn't have left you"

Witness

I once came to fix you.
Now I come to witness you.
To hold the trembling pieces you've carried
since the man that fathered you refused to claim you.
You said,
"If I had found you earlier,
maybe my life would be different."
But love—
You found me now.
And that should be enough.

I've been sitting at the intersection
of your pain and your potential,
planting seeds in the cracks of your belief system,
hoping something beautiful might bloom.
You say I talk like I'm distant,
but this isn't distance.
This is the language of someone
who stayed after the crash.
Who read every chapter of your ache
and still called it sacred.

Now I'm becoming a mirror you're not ready to see
yourself in

A projection that's doesn't blink or bend under the
weight of your projection

I'm telling you:
You can rewrite the script.
You can reroute the ache.
You can break the chain.
But I can't drag you out your cage

Your trauma built a fortress,
but I brought down the walls
so you could hopefully feel what love
without condition tastes like after the fall
It tastes like truth.
It tastes like boundaries.
It tastes like "I see you, even when you hide"

You said your hurt is different,
but pain doesn't ask for credentials.
One father had his gun,
another father had his silence,
and both left people
searching for meaning in mileage
Of their cars to go far
& Hoping—
we can make new dreams.
We can name new stars.

We can break every chain,
but not by forgetting who we are,
but by finding truth where the wound once lived.
I don't write all this
because I'm angry.
I say all this
because I love you.
And a love this real
refuses to coddle your cage.
So here I am,
not to rescue,
But to remind you:
you were never really broken;
just buried.
Under all the circumstances of your life.
And I came with shovels
full of sunlight.

Star-Spangled Justice

One day
I will tell the stars about you
about how you wrapped yourself to my constellation
about how I wrapped myself to yours
about how we fastened ourselves into each other's
futures
the same way Orion's belt is whipped amidst the
luminous orbs
so close, yet still so far
You knew me
I could tell
by the way you sat in the center of my eyes
like twinkling stardust—
Making sense of the milky way.

The moon inspired our progression,
made sense of our secret obsessions
And we transited the night skies
as if we wouldn't ever see the sun
but the sun knew the truth of our constellation
and while we were star crossed lovers
we were lovers, nonetheless.
Lounging lovers, under cosmic covers
Has no one ever explained to you

what playing with the stars can do?

I've done this before...
Imposed my inception,
designed by spirits deception.
Your passion was like bottomless waters
fixed and immovable,
deep & desirable
And my adoration to swim surpassed
my effortless enjoyment to breathe

I just love to delve into deep-seated waters
without an oxygen tank
Call me an adrenaline junky, but I was in love
So I sank
I was inclined to drown in the bittersweet symphonies
of your exalted and salted seas...

Who will resuscitate my breath,
hence my heart can begin to beat?

For our assumptions were earthly manners
that our celestial bodies became all too acquainted with.
And when we undo the cords between us
what kind of shift will become of this karmic rift?
So yes,
One day I will tell the stars about you.

As if they don't already know...
And tell them matters of the heart
to explain why our seeds were sown.
And clarify any misdeeds that felt so good
Because any sensation to a numb soul
felt the same as love would

Your stirring of the spectacle that was my spirit
was like being sent on a space odyssey
It's cold, but its weightless
and boy, did it expand this universe.
So I balance the moon with the sun in the stars
and call this liberated love,
no longer ours
in the same
way.
Yet,
Love
remains.

Karma Coins

This Love
It came in a fleeting second,
Bound to the second hand of a running clock,
you see, it was temporary
it was meant to fall off
I was only
checking my time
when I looked down at my watch
Only to find
that it was a little bit off
My fingers,
wrapped around the winding crown
twisting to fix it right
I hadn't realized, that well,
This Love,
it had hit the minute hand
and now it was holding on so tight.

This Love
It came in a fleeting second,
And it was holding on for minutes now
We had just left the park
And yeah, I had gotten home safe
Only now, Love was ticking through my mind

and my heart was in a race
A race against the clock
where love sat so restlessly
yet, not making a flinching move
as the tock of the clock hit incessantly
you see, we were aiming for longevity
That night, I took my watch off
and it rang in my mind *every* minute
To the point where I hadn't realized
that as the clock turned and my eyes fell into REM
my love was already there hanging out on the limb.

This love
It came in a fleeting second,
And it was hanging on for hours now...
When I woke up the next day
I put my watch back on,
and I *loved* the way it looked today
because Love was here to stay!
No more, *hey baby, won't you come my way*
So I got in my car, and I hit the stereo
and now I *think I'm in love with my radio,*
because as I sang sweet love songs
I hadn't realized that love had clung to my digital analog
Now,
hours turned into days,
and

days turned into weeks,
cause Lord knows I drive everyday
comin' out your way
you see, I was wrapped around its heart
And I guess, Love was wrapped around mine too
Because Love was wrapped around *my* time
and if time is precious, then *sheesh!* baby,
you...
you must be a diamond
because there's nothing I wouldn't do to fill my time and
plans up with having You.

This Love
It came in a fleeting second,
and it stayed.

For *too* damn long.
Now don't get me wrong,
This Love,
it taught me a lot of lessons and life points
it had me stackin' up on Karma coins
This love—
it led me all the way up to this point.
To the here and now,
and after all the ups and downs
When I think of the past, I am humbled
And when I think of the future, I am blessed

I've got nothing but love and respect
for this old, soulful watch
But next time,
Love,
You won't come on a clock because
True Love,
is timeless.

Tic Tac Toe

Cross my t's
And bat my eyes
Play tic tac toe
All over my body
Uncross my legs
And circle my thighs
Caress my vibes
Undress my rhymes
They're here,
Slowing all time
With no fear,
Showing all shine
Feel the earth turn
Hear the stars burn
Near to me
Dear to me
Soft words like Flowetry
Sit back in this mold with me
Post with me
Dose with me
Mess around a lil bit
And grow old with me

Davey's Locker

I'm a "*I like what I see*" and then wait for you to notice
type of girl...
I'm a "*give you one good hint*" and let you handle the
rest kinda girl.
I know it sounds shy but,
I'm a take-all-you-can-give
and a give-all-you-can-take kinda girl,
And then
accidentally do a little more,
be a lil more,
give a little more,
just because I love you kind of girl...

But first, I need to know that you need me,
nah, that you truly *see* me.
That when you see these eyes
and they don't just run across your mind
But they sting you in the dark.
And capture your heart.
Look at me—
Deep.
My eyes are not shallow or weak
They're the key to my chested treasure
I invite *you* to swim in my seas

Enter Davey's locker
You will not come out alive
You will drown your "I"
and float up a whole new vibe

Wounds

I told myself to not let them see my wounds

And then I let you kiss me,

and you said,

"Look, you don't have any."

A Snapshot of My Senses

It's summertime
and I am on the 210 freeway
With a flask of 210 degree coffee
Basically, Burnin' up

I am rolling hills
And blue skies
Without bound while pouring cups

I am lipstick stains
On secret cigs
and hot ceramic mugs

I am purple amethyst
Picking up powder at the post office
Divine feminine signed with love

I am both On Call and Happy Alone
By the Red Morning Light in a Talihina Sky
the Queen of all Leon's Kings

I am crimson and clover
Over and over
Crimson and Clover, covered in rings

I am past present and Future
Love song. L-o-v-e-e-e, and affection
A series of drawn out flings

I am a goddess in the flesh, call me 'Hova
An accumulation of hard knocks
Sad tunes she sweetly sings

I am scatterbrained and Helter-Skelter
Running *away* from shelter
I'd rather Love Reign O'er Me

I am infinitely inspired
And crafting my creativity
Through the fleeting feeling of moments relativity

I am roaming rhymes,
messy metaphors,
and sometimes too clean cut

Alliteration and consonance rule my mind
Hear me once loud and clear before I Shut
Up! Like black eyed peas

Alluding to the silence we make
as we cross our T's

Cause no one wants to eat them things

But we do eat all the love we make
& I sense my quiet can be a bit too loud
When I seize up with each breath we take,
I know I'll make you proud

And speaking of seizures, I mean caesura—
Because I'm sure my breaks in cadence
Provides you peace amongst the petty things...

I am omnipresent and omnipotent
When I'm tuned into a musical focus
A weathered woman wearing Pretty Wings

I am unapologetically,
Relentlessly,
Notoriously B.I.G.,
Me

Two Things Can Be True at Once

Are you my undoing?

Or my divine truth?

You are both.

Set me free...

Let me loose...

Light Switches

I've traded in my light switches for
gradually rotating knobs for the time being
It's time I started dimming down my inhibitions
and brightening up my believing
I've come to know light switches all too well
In how they shut light out in the blink of an eye,
so fast, not even time could tell
I'm tryna get acquainted
with the thoughtful meditations
that make light swell
Flipping up and down is like activating your karma,
because what goes up must come down
While spinning round and round is like a wheel of
dharma,
because a lesson learned is a lesson sound

My love used to be like a light switch;
one more false move and I'm shutting you out
Pitch black love, while I pitch back the ball
you threw at my doubt
Love is no longer up for trial
No more switching the light on faces
like a detective waiting on denial
So, I'm trading in my light switches for

gradually rotating knobs that think & move more
critically
To set the mood and set the tone
to get precisely in my zone

My mental health used to be like a light switch;
One more thing added to my laundry list
and I just might blow up all of it
Or feigning a smile to make coffee for awhile
I'm so weary of the all too bright house lights going up
And then telling the sound of darkness to shut up
So, I'm trading in my light switches for
gradually rotating knobs that can find a balance
No more losing my grip on an out of my hand's
occurrence
I seek my solitude in silence

So, when you step in my room and the light
is neither off nor shining bright
Know that I'm doing the work
to find the control in making things right

Love of Sun

What if,
Your issues could be solved with the addition of one
single factor.
Allow a consideration, if you will.
Love.

What if,
All that was in place of happiness—
Joy.

All that was in place of loneliness—
Solitude.

All that was in place of
longing and waiting—
patience.

All that was in place of
search and discovery—
enlightenment.

Allow me to illustrate—
the Sun.

It does not flicker of fluorescence, providing glimpses of happiness, given the turn of a switch.
Rather it eternally beams, glows, and warms all that it touches through its internal radiance;
a true source of joy.

It does not sit in a seeming loneliness in the stratosphere above our heads.
Rather, it sits in the solitude of God's blue-painted astral living room,
an example of meditation.

It does not wait on its friendly acquaintance of night, counting the seconds to illuminate once more.
Rather, it rises and sets with its devoted partner,
the Moon,
and shimmers of patience upon every earthly eye to see,
an enduring presence.

It does not search to discover the eyes of its unfaithful watchers in hopes of their appreciation.
But it basks in the enlightenment of its higher purpose,
and dutifully guides each of us to the road of our own.

This is the love we are all yearning to know.
And as the sons of love,

we feel the love
of sun.

www.ingramcontent.com/pod-product-compliance
Lightning Source LLC
Chambersburg PA
CBHW060349050426
42449CB00011B/2891